Bread

Saviour Pirotta

A⁺

First published in 2004 by Hodder Wayland,
an imprint of Hodder Children's Books,
338 Euston Road, London NW1 3BH
This edition published under license from Hodder Wayland. All rights reserved.

Text copyright © 2004 Saviour Pirotta

Language consultant: Andrew Burrell
Subject consultant: Carol Ballard
Design: Perry Tate Design
Picture research: Glass Onion Pictures

Published in the United States by Smart Apple Media
1980 Lookout Drive, North Mankato, Minnesota 56003

U.S. publication copyright © 2005 Smart Apple Media
International copyright reserved in all countries. No part of this book may be
reproduced in any form without written permission from the publisher.

Library of Congress Cataloging-in-Publication Data

Pirotta, Saviour.
Bread / by Saviour Pirotta.
p. cm. — (Starters)
Includes index.
ISBN 1-58340-563-1
1. Bread—Juvenile literature. I. Title. II. Series.

TX769.P525 2004
664'.7523—dc22   2004041703

9 8 7 6 5 4 3 2 1

The publishers would like to thank the following for allowing us to reproduce their
pictures in this book: Angela Hampton Family Life Picture Library; title page, 17
(bottom right) / Cephas; 4 / Corbis; 11 (bottom), 12 (bottom), 22 (bottom), 23 (top) /
Foodpix; 12, 23 (bottom) / Getty; 5 (bottom), 7, 8, 10 / Hodder Wayland Picture
Library; contents page, 9, 17 (top left and right, bottom left), 18, 19, 20 (top), 21 (top) /
Stockfood; cover; 6, 7, 11 (top), 12 (top), 13, 15 (top), 20 (bottom), 22 (top) / Topham
Picturepoint; 15 (bottom), 16 (Chapman) / Travel Ink; 21 (bottom)

Contents

Delicious bread

How could we live without bread?

We toast it for breakfast
in the morning.

Eggs and toast make a tasty breakfast!

We use bread to
make sandwiches
at lunchtime.

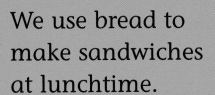

Sandwiches can have
many different
delicious fillings.

We might DIP bread
in soup, or bake it
with cheese for
supper.

Which grain?

Most bread is made from grain, the seed-like fruit of special grasses. Bread can be made from rye, millet, oats, corn, or wheat.

These crackers are made from different types of grain.

Rye bread is very popular in northern Europe.

The most common bread is made from wheat.

Harvest time

Farmers grow wheat in **enormous** fields. When it is ripe, they collect the grain with a special machine called a combine.

This wheat is ready to be harvested.

The combine cuts the wheat with sharp, turning blades. It also separates the grain from the stalks. The grain is saved, and the stalks are dropped onto the ground.

The combine pours the grain into the trailer.

At the mill

The farmer sends the grain to the flourmill. At the mill, it is piled HIGH, ready to be cleaned many times to make sure there is no dirt in it.

The clean grain is passed through metal rollers that **CRUSH** and grind the grain into flour.

The fresh, new flour is collected in large sacks.

To the bakery

From the mill, the flour goes to the bakery. The baker mixes it with water, yeast, and a little sugar and salt.

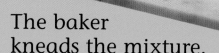

The baker kneads the mixture.

The yeast in the dough makes it grow **bigger**. The baker cuts it into pieces to make loaves.

The loaves are baked in the oven until they are golden brown and ready to eat.

Mmmm, that bread smells delicious!

The bread factory

At some big bakeries, the bread is made by machines. First, the dough is made in **GIANT** mixers.

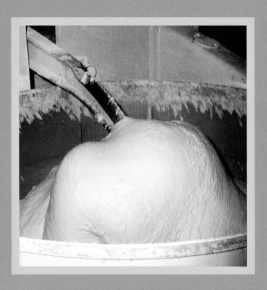

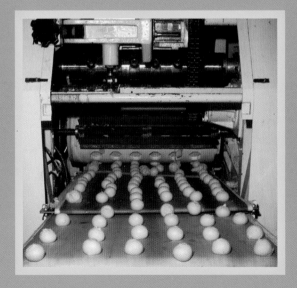

Then, another machine splits the dough into loaves and rolls.

These rolls are ready for the oven.

The bread slowly travels through the oven. When it comes out on the other side, the bread is baked. It is ready to be sliced and packaged.

Wrapping the bread keeps it fresh.

Let's get some bread

Before long, the bread is in the grocery store for people to buy. **Mmm**, the smell of fresh bread brings people to the bread counter.

This man is buying a French loaf.

There are so many kinds of bread to choose from. **Long** and crusty. *Round* and soft. Square tin loaves. Sliced loaves in bags. White bread, brown bread, and whole grain!

foccacia

bagel

It makes your tummy growl with hunger.

croissant

whole grain loaf

Bread is good for you

Bread is not
only delicious,
it is also very good
for you. Bread gives
you energy. It helps
keep you healthy.

Bread helps you
to run, jump,
and play.

Bread also contains fiber. Fiber helps your blood flow around your body. It also helps push waste through your body.

For extra fiber, whole grain bread is best.

Bread around the world

People all over the world enjoy bread.

In India, people eat *round* nan bread and chapattis with curry and rice.

In Turkey, people stuff pockets of pita bread with cheese, vegetables, or slices of meat.

In Mexico, people wrap spicy meat, beans, and vegetables in tortillas.

Pizza is a **FLAT** bread from Italy that is covered with different toppings. It is enjoyed by people in many countries.

Pizza is delicious!

Celebrate!

Bread helps us celebrate, too.
In some countries, people
eat a special bread at Easter.
It is made in beautiful shapes
and decorated with eggs, nuts,
or fruit.

Jewish people celebrate the festival of Passover
with special, flat bread.

Christmas bread can come in special shapes. Sometimes it has frosting and fruit on top.

It is not surprising that bread is one of the most popular foods in the world.

Glossary and index

Combine   A machine that picks and cleans grain crops. **8, 9**

Dough   A stiff mixture of flour and liquid that is baked to become bread. **12, 14**

Fiber   The rough part of food, including the outer shell of grains. **19**

Flour   A powder made by crushing grains and removing the outer shells. **11, 12**

Flourmill   A place where grains are turned into flour. **10**

Grain   The seeds of food plants. **6, 8, 9, 10, 11**

Grind   To crush into powder. **11**

Knead   To make bread dough smooth by pressing it again and again. **12**

Ripe   Ready for picking. **8**

Whole grain bread   Bread that is made by using the whole grain instead of crushed flour. **17, 19**

Yeast   A special ingredient that makes bread and cakes soft and fluffy. **12**